First hundred words in Japanese

Heather Amery

Illustrated by Stephen Cartwright

Translation and pronunciation guide by
Quarto Translations

Designed by Mike Olley and Jan McCafferty

 There is a little yellow duck to find in every picture.

いま　*ima*　The living room

おとうさん
otōsan　Daddy

おかあさん
okāsan　Mummy

おとこのこ
otoko no ko　boy

おんなのこ
onna no ko girl

あかちゃん
akachan baby

いぬ
inu dog

ねこ
neko cat

ようふく　*yōfuku*　Clothes

くつ
kutsu　shoes

パンツ
pantsu　pants

ジャンパー
janpā　jumper

ベスト
besuto vest

ズボン
zubon trousers

ティーシャツ
tīshatsu t-shirt

ソックス
sokkusu socks

あさごはん　*asagohan*　Breakfast

パン
pan　bread

ぎゅうにゅう
gyūnyū　milk

たまご
tamago　eggs

りんご

ringo   apple

オレンジ

orenji   orange

バナナ

banana   banana

だいどころ *daidokoro* The kitchen

テーブル

tēburu table

いす

isu chair

おさら

osara plate

8

ナイフ
naifu   knife

フォーク
fōku   fork

スプーン
supūn   spoon

カップ
kappu   cup

おもちゃ　*omocha*　Toys

うま
uma　horse

ひつじ
hitsuji　sheep

うし
ushi　cow

10

にわとり
niwatori hen

ぶた
buta pig

きしゃ
kisha train

つみき
tsumiki blocks

ほうもん　*hōmon*　On a visit

おばあさん
obāsan　Granny

おじいさん
ojīsan　Grandpa

スリッパ
surippa　slippers

コート

kōto coat

ドレス

doresu dress

ぼうし

bōshi hat

こうえん　*kōen*　The park

き
ki　tree

はな
hana　flower

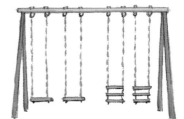
ぶらんこ
buranko　swings

まり
mari　ball

すべりだい
suberidai slide

ブーツ
būtsu boots

とり
tori bird

ふね
fune boat

15

とおり *tōri* The street

くるま
kuruma car

じてんしゃ
jitensha bicycle

ひこうき
hikōki plane

トラック

torakku　truck

バス

basu　bus

いえ

ie　house

パーティー *pātī* The party

ふうせん
fūsen balloon

ケーキ
kēki cake

とけい
tokei clock

アイスクリーム
aisu kurīmu
ice cream

さかな
sakana fish

ビスケット
bisuketto biscuits

おかし
okashi sweets

プール   *pūru*   The swimming pool

うで

ude   arm

て

te   hand

あし

ashi   leg

あし
ashi feet

つまさき
tsumasaki toes

あたま
atama head

おしり
oshiri bottom

こういしつ *kōishitsu* The changing room

くち

kuchi mouth

め

me eyes

みみ

mimi ears

はな
hana　nose

かみ
kami　hair

くし
kushi　comb

ブラシ
burashi　brush

23

おみせ *omise* The shop

あか
aka red

あお
ao blue

みどり
midori green

24

きいろ

ki-iro yellow

ピンク

pinku pink

しろ

shiro white

くろ

kuro black

よくしつ *yokushitsu* The bathroom

せっけん

sekken soap

タオル

taoru towel

トイレ

toire toilet

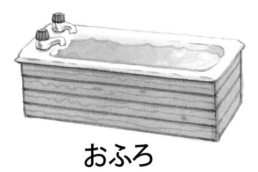

おふろ
ofuro bath

おなか
onaka tummy

あひる
ahiru duck

27

しんしつ   *shinshitsu*   The bedroom

ベッド

beddo   bed

ランプ

ranpu   lamp

まど

mado   window

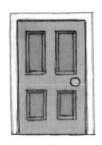   

ドア
doa door

ほん
hon book

にんぎょう
ningyō doll

テディー ベア
tedībea teddy

Match the words to the pictures

バナナ
banana

まど
mado

さかな
sakana

たまご
tamago

まり
mari

ジャンパー
janpā

ベスト
besuto

ソックス
sokkusu

りんご
ringo

テディーベア
tedībea

いぬ
inu

とけい
tokei

ケーキ
kēki

ナイフ
naifu

ねこ
neko

アイスクリーム
aisu kurīmu

くるま
kuruma

オレンジ
orenji

にんぎょう
ningyō

あひる
ahiru

ぶた
buta

ほん
hon

ランプ
ranpu

ぼうし
bōshi

ブーツ
būtsu

フォーク
fōku

うし
ushi

きしゃ
kisha

テーブル
tēburu

ぎゅうにゅう
gyūnyū

31

かず *kazu*   Numbers

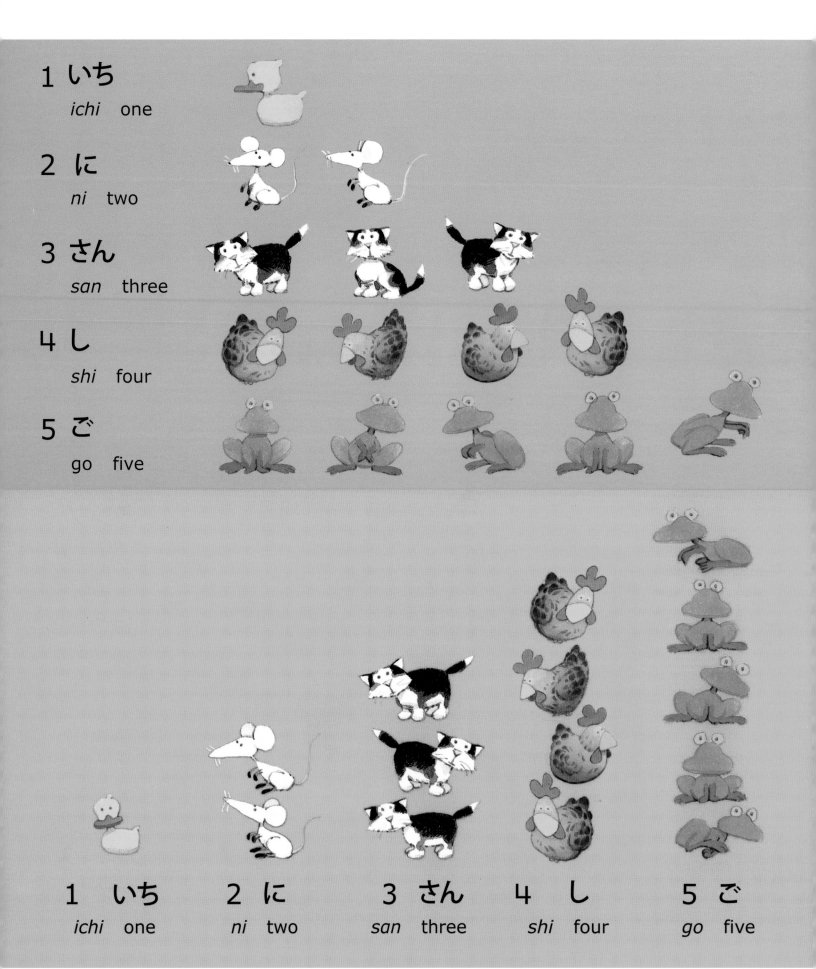

1 いち
ichi one

2 に
ni two

3 さん
san three

4 し
shi four

5 ご
go five

1 いち
ichi one

2 に
ni two

3 さん
san three

4 し
shi four

5 ご
go five

About Japanese writing

The words in this book are written in simple Japanese signs, called *kana*. Each *kana* represents a syllable. (A syllable is part of a word that is a separate sound, for example, "today" has two syllables: "to" and "day".) Below you can see all the *kana* signs and find out which sounds they represent.

Japanese has two sets of *kana* signs, called *hiragana* and *katakana*. *Hiragana* signs are used for the traditional sounds of Japanese. *Katakana* signs are used for words that Japanese has borrowed from other languages, such as "taoru", borrowed from the English word "towel".

Next to each *kana* you can see a guide to how it is said. In the book, each Japanese word is shown in the same way, that is, in *kana* with a guide to help you say it, based on the guides on page 34.

Hiragana

Kana	Sound	Kana	Sound	Kana	Sound	Kana	Sound	Kana	Sound
あ	a	い	i	う	u	え	e	お	o
か	ka	き	ki	く	ku	け	ke	こ	ko
が	ga	ぎ	gi	ぐ	gu	げ	ge	ご	go
さ	sa	し	shi	す	su	せ	se	そ	so
ざ	za	じ	ji	ず	zu	ぜ	ze	ぞ	zo
た	ta	ち	chi	つ	tsu	て	te	と	to
だ	da			づ	zu	で	de	ど	do
な	na	に	ni	ぬ	nu	ね	ne	の	no
は	ha	ひ	hi	ふ	fu	へ	he	ほ	ho
ば	ba	び	bi	ぶ	bu	べ	be	ぼ	bo
ぱ	pa	ぴ	pi	ぷ	pu	ぺ	pe	ぽ	po
ま	ma	み	mi	む	mu	め	me	も	mo
や	ya			ゆ	yu			よ	yo
ら	ra	り	ri	る	ru	れ	re	ろ	ro
わ	wa							を	(w)o
ん	n								

Katakana

Kana	Sound	Kana	Sound	Kana	Sound	Kana	Sound	Kana	Sound
ア	a	イ	i	ウ	u	エ	e	オ	o
カ	ka	キ	ki	ク	ku	ケ	ke	コ	ko
ガ	ga	ギ	gi	グ	gu	ゲ	ge	ゴ	go
サ	sa	シ	shi	ス	su	セ	se	ソ	so
ザ	za	ジ	ji	ズ	zu	ゼ	ze	ゾ	zo
タ	ta	チ	chi	ツ	tsu	テ	te	ト	to
ダ	da			ヅ	zu	デ	de	ド	do
ナ	na	ニ	ni	ヌ	nu	ネ	ne	ド	no
ハ	ha	ヒ	hi	フ	fu	へ	he	ホ	ho
バ	ba	ビ	bi	ブ	bu	べ	be	ボ	bo
パ	pa	ピ	pi	プ	pu	ペ	pe	ポ	po
マ	ma	ミ	mi	ム	mu	メ	me	モ	mo
ヤ	ya			ユ	yu			ヨ	yo
ラ	ra	リ	ri	ル	ru	レ	re	ロ	ro
ワ	wa							ヲ	(w)o
ン	n								

Kanji

Japanese also uses more complicated signs, called *kanji* or "characters". Each *kanji* is a symbol for a word or idea. There are thousands of *kanji* and it takes a few years to learn them, so it is best to start with *kana*, learning a few of these at a time.

Word list

In this list you will find all the words in this book in the alphabetical order of the English words. Next to each English word is the Japanese word written in *kana* signs, and then a guide that shows you how to say it.

Following these hints will help you say the *kana* signs in a really Japanese way. Remember, a line over a letter shows the sound is long.

say *a* like *a* in *a*pple
say *e* like *e* in *e*nd
say *i* like *i* in k*i*tchen
say *o* like the *o* in h*o*t
say *u* like *u* in p*u*t

say *ā* like *a* in f*a*ther
say *ē* like *ee* in b*ee*
say *ī* like *ee* in b*ee*
say *ō* like the *o* in c*o*rn
say *ū* like *oo* in f*oo*d

Say the other letters as if they were part of an English word, but remember:

say *r* as a soft *r* sound, halfway between an *l* and an *r*

say *g* as in *g*arden

the *(w)o* sound is shown with the *w* in brackets because you sometimes say *wo* and sometimes just *o*. In the book the pronunciation guide will make it clear which sound to make

the *fu* sound is halfway between *foo* and *hoo*

if you see the *n* sound on its own (at the bottom of each list), say it through your nose, as if you have a cold

In English, many words have a part that you stress, or say louder. For example in the word *today*, you stress *day*. In Japanese, you say each part of the word with the same stress.

apple	りんご	*ringo*
arm	うで	*ude*
baby	あかちゃん	*akachan*
ball	まり	*mari*
balloon	ふうせん	*fūsen*
banana	バナナ	*banana*
bath	おふろ	*ofuro*
bathroom	よくしつ	*yokushitsu*
bed	ベッド	*beddo*
bedroom	しんしつ	*shinshitsu*
bicycle	じてんしゃ	*jitensha*
bird	とり	*tori*
biscuits	ビスケット	*bisuketto*
black	くろ	*kuro*
blocks	つみき	*tsumiki*
blue	あお	*ao*
boat	ふね	*fune*
book	ほん	*hon*
boots	ブーツ	*būtsu*
bottom	おしり	*oshiri*
boy	おとこのこ	*otoko no ko*
bread	パン	*pan*
breakfast	あさごはん	*asagohan*
brush	ブラシ	*burashi*
bus	バス	*basu*
cake	ケーキ	*kēki*

car	くるま	*kuruma*
cat	ねこ	*neko*
chair	いす	*isu*
changing room	こういしつ	*kōishitsu*
clock	とけい	*tokei*
clothes	ようふく	*yōfuku*
coat	コート	*kōto*
comb	くし	*kushi*
cow	うし	*ushi*
cup	カップ	*kappu*
Daddy	おとうさん	*otōsan*
dog	いぬ	*inu*
doll	にんぎょう	*ningyō*
door	ドア	*doa*
dress	ドレス	*doresu*
duck	あひる	*ahiru*
ears	みみ	*mimi*
egg / eggs	たまご	*tamago*
eyes	め	*me*
feet	あし	*ashi*
fish	さかな	*sakana*
five	ご	*go*
flower	はな	*hana*
fork	フォーク	*fōku*
four	し	*shi*